Who Was
Clara Barton?

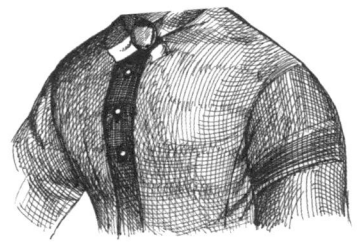

Who Was Clara Barton?

by Stephanie Spinner

illustrated by David Groff

Penguin Workshop

For Linda Dovydenas—SS

For my children, Alana and Elise and Grant—DG

PENGUIN WORKSHOP
An Imprint of Penguin Random House LLC, New York

Visit us online at www.penguinrandomhouse.com.

Library of Congress Control Number: 2015410122

ISBN 9780448479538   10 9 8 7 6 5 4 3 2

Part of the *What Is Science & Technology?* Boxed Set, ISBN 9780593090138

Contents

Who Was Clara Barton?.........................1

Six Mothers and Fathers.........................4

A Born Teacher.........................11

Bold Steps.........................24

Angel of the Battlefield.........................35

Speaking Out.........................48

The Long Campaign.........................56

Fire, Famine, and Flood.........................69

A Heart without Borders.........................87

Clara's Legacy.........................95

Timelines.........................102

Bibliography.........................104

Who Was
Clara Barton?

In 1833, when Clara Barton was eleven, her
brother David fell off the roof of the barn on her
family's farm. He didn't break any bones, but
he did get very sick. Clara decided to take care
of him. She cleaned his wounds, changed his

bandages, and brought him his meals. For two years she almost never left his side.

By the time David recovered, Clara was very good at nursing. Everything she'd done to help her brother seemed to come naturally to her. So when dozens of children in her Massachusetts town came down with smallpox, Clara nursed them, too. She knew that she might get smallpox, but that didn't stop her. The children needed her help.

Over the course of her long, busy life, Clara Barton never stopped helping and healing people. She started schools for poor children, nursed wounded soldiers during the Civil War, and fought long and hard to bring the Red Cross to the United States. Under her leadership, the Red Cross won fame for its treatment of disaster victims and

set new standards for public service. Barton also transformed the nursing profession, strengthened the women's movement, and inspired volunteer organizations all over the world. Once a shy small-town girl, Clara Barton became a true force for change. She was a woman to be reckoned with.

Chapter 1
Six Mothers and Fathers

Clarissa Harlow Barton, born in North Oxford, Massachusetts, on Christmas Day of 1821, was her parents' fifth child. She was the baby of the family, and her two sisters and two brothers were much older than she was. In Clara's household, everybody, not just her parents, told her what to do. It was almost like having six parents instead of two.

But Clara was lucky—five of the six were interested in taking good care of her and making sure she learned the important things in life. Her father, Captain Stephen Barton, taught her about military history. Once an army officer in the Northwest Indian War of 1785–1795, he liked to sit by the fire and talk about his adventures. Clara would spend hours acting out different battles with him, which they both enjoyed very much.

Clara's sisters, Dolly and Sarah, already were teaching in local Massachusetts schools when she was born. They loved books and poetry, and taught Clara to read when she was three. Sarah read poetry to her every night. Even as a small child, Clara was just as drawn to books as they were.

Dolly and Sarah also taught her the things little girls had to know at that time: cooking, sewing, and cleaning. Because the Bartons lived on a farm, Clara was doing chores from the time she could toddle. She fed the chickens and gathered their eggs. She picked vegetables for the family's supper.

She helped to make soap. And, of course, she
milked cows—just about anybody growing up on
a farm learned how to do that.

But there were some things that little girls in the 1820s did not learn how to do. Galloping bareback (without a saddle) on an untrained colt was one. Using men's tools, like a hammer and a screwdriver, was another. Tying strong, reliable knots was a third. And throwing a ball hard and straight like a boy? Never.

Even so, Clara's big brothers, Stephen and David, taught her all those things and more. Stephen was very good with numbers, and he became Clara's math teacher. "Multiplication, division, subtraction, halves, quarters, and wholes, soon ceased to be a mystery," she later wrote. David, the athlete of the family, taught her to love animals—especially horses—as much as he did. He encouraged her to play outside in the woods like a tomboy, rather than in the house with dolls. Perhaps because he ignored the rules that kept nineteenth-century girls inside, busily being "little women," he was something of a hero to Clara.

The one Barton who didn't show much interest in raising young Clara was her mother, Sarah.

A hardworking, outspoken woman, Sarah Barton was in favor of ending slavery and giving women the vote. Like her husband, she was a firm believer in equal rights for all.

Sarah left Clara's day-to-day care to the other Bartons. But she still worried about her daughter's extreme shyness, which worsened as she got older. She even consulted L.N. Fowler, a visiting phrenologist, about her "difficult" daughter. What could timid Clara, now sixteen, possibly do with her life?

Phrenology was based on the false notion that the bumps and ridges on a person's skull revealed that person's strengths and weaknesses. Now that Fowler had seen Clara, what advice could he give?

To overcome her shyness, said Fowler, Clara should teach summer school. And he was absolutely right.

Chapter 2
A Born Teacher

Clara was not happy about Fowler's advice. Teaching a roomful of strangers sounded like torture to her. But a year later, she found herself standing in the one-room North Oxford schoolhouse, facing forty pupils. The oldest students, teenage boys "as tall and nearly as old

as myself," as she wrote later, didn't hide the fact that they would rather be elsewhere. But if they thought they could rattle the new schoolmarm because she was only seventeen, they were mistaken. As she began to read aloud on that first

day, Clara's painful shyness vanished. She started to enjoy herself, and so did the class. A few days later during recess, she proved that she could throw a ball straight and hard. She could outrun them, too. Amazing!

That summer, Clara's natural teaching skills surprised everyone, including herself. Her classes were lively yet disciplined, and the students were clearly happy to be there. The word spread, and she began to get job offers from other towns. The following year she taught summer school again, this time in nearby Charlton, Massachusetts. Her salary was two dollars a week. This was normal for summer school, which was usually taught by women. Men were the ones who almost always taught the full school year, and they were paid more.

In 1840 the local school board offered Clara a position for the full school year, but at summer-school wages. Clara calmly told the board she would take the job, but only if she were paid as much as a man. The board agreed. Hearing of this small victory, Sarah Barton must have been pleased. Her timid daughter was learning to stand up for herself.

Over the next ten years, Clara taught at many local schools. More than anything, she wanted her students to get the best education they could. So when she learned that many poor families right in her hometown had no school to send their children to, she resolved to help them. Like her parents, Clara believed in equal opportunity for everyone.

With her brother Stephen, now a millowner in Oxford, Clara raised money to build a school for the mill workers' children. While teaching there, she worked especially hard with Irish and German immigrant children to improve their English.

Meanwhile, she yearned to continue her own education. In 1850 she took a bold step: She enrolled at Clinton Liberal Institute. It was one of the few coeducational academies in America.

It was also two hundered miles from Oxford, and Clara had never left home before. But she made the trip to Clinton, and she was never again afraid to travel.

Clara took courses in history, philosophy, advanced mathematics, and foreign languages. She studied hard and made some good friends. But she had only enough money to pay for three terms at the academy, so in 1851 she returned home. Sadly, "home" was not as Clara had left it.

While she was away, her mother had died suddenly, and now Clara missed her very much.

Her aging father had moved in with her brother David. She didn't have much money. She was terribly lonely, and anxious about her future. Worst of all, as she confided to her diary, "I was not needed."

For all these reasons, Clara was quick to accept an invitation to visit fellow Clinton students Charles and Mary Norton in Hightstown, New Jersey. The Nortons had a busy social life, and at first Clara was delighted to spend all her time with them. Mary, who was only sixteen, looked up to her. Charles, twenty-one, flirted with her. Their parents kept asking Clara to stay on.

But after a few weeks with the Nortons, Clara grew tired of dinners and tea parties. She wanted something useful to do. The opportunity came with an unexpected question from Mr. Norton: Was she interested in teaching at a boys' school in Cedarville, New Jersey, just a few miles away? She was.

Clara had never told any of her fellow students at Clinton about her teaching experience. She wanted badly to fit in, and at twenty-nine she was much older than the other students. But they never guessed it because Clara was petite, soft-spoken, and girlish. So when she tamed the rough, unruly Cedarville schoolboys in a matter of days, the Nortons were amazed. Miss Clara Barton was a miracle worker!

If she dreamed of working miracles, Clara kept that to herself. But she was always open about wanting to help people, and very soon she got the chance.

CHILD LABOR IN CLARA'S TIME

IN 1821, WHEN CLARA BARTON WAS BORN, MANY AMERICAN CHILDREN STARTED WORKING WHEN THEY WERE AS YOUNG AS FIVE OR SIX YEARS OLD. SOME WORKED TWELVE HOURS A DAY OR MORE. THEIR JOBS—IN TEXTILE MILLS, FACTORIES, CANNERIES, AND COAL MINES, ON FARMS AND CITY TENEMENTS—PAID ALMOST NOTHING. THE WORK WAS OFTEN DANGEROUS. IF THEY BECAME SICK OR INJURED, THEY WEREN'T PAID AT ALL. THROUGHOUT THE 1800S, MOST WORKING CHILDREN COULDN'T READ OR WRITE BECAUSE THEY DIDN'T GO TO SCHOOL. MANY SCHOOLS CHARGED FEES THAT POOR FAMILIES COULDN'T AFFORD.

AND THERE
WERE NO LAWS
REQUIRING
CHILDREN TO GET
AN EDUCATION.
CLARA'S
HOME STATE OF
MASSACHUSETTS
PASSED THE
FIRST CHILD
LABOR LAW IN

1836. UNDER THE NEW LAW, CHILDREN UNDER
AGE FIFTEEN HAD TO GO TO SCHOOL FOR AT
LEAST THREE MONTHS A YEAR. IN 1842 ANOTHER
NEW MASSACHUSETTS LAW KEPT CHILDREN FROM
WORKING MORE THAN TEN HOURS A DAY.

THE FIRST FEDERAL CHILD LABOR LAW, CALLED
THE FAIR LABOR STANDARDS ACT, DID NOT GO
INTO EFFECT UNTIL 1938.

Chapter 3
Bold Steps

In May of 1852, Clara was in Bordentown, New Jersey, a few miles from the Nortons' home in Hightstown. Noticing several groups of boys on the street, she asked why they weren't in school.

The answer was, "Lady, there is no school for us."

But, Clara thought, *there should be!* Schools were not free in New Jersey, as they were in Massachusetts, and that seemed very unfair to her. Then and there, Clara decided to take action. She arranged a meeting with the Bordentown school board and asked its members to open a free school. She told them what she had accomplished in Oxford and Cedarville and promised to do the same for them. Moreover, if they opened a free school, she would teach there without pay.

The board accepted her offer. The very next day, an old school building was reopened. Over

the next few weeks it was cleaned and furnished with benches, maps, and blackboards. In July, Clara greeted her first class—six boys. She was friendly and relaxed and quickly put them at their ease, answering their questions about the different countries on the maps with stories, not dry facts. The following day there were twenty boys in the classroom, and in two weeks, there were fifty-five. Girls began to come, too. The new school was getting crowded!

Within a few months, it was so full that the
board hired Clara's friend Fanny Childs to teach
there, too. And the townspeople were so pleased

that they voted to pay Clara and Fanny each $250 a year—an excellent salary at the time.

Everyone was happy, especially Clara. By the end of the year, the school that had opened with only six students had two hundred, and four hundred more children were waiting to attend! To Clara's delight, the townspeople now fully supported free education. They voted to build another, bigger school for all six hundred students, with two stories and separate rooms for each grade. It was a wonderful triumph for her after all her hard work. Her future in Bordentown looked very bright.

But when Schoolhouse One, as the new school was called, was ready to open, Clara was told that she would not be its principal. The job was considered too important and too hard for a woman. The school board had hired a man instead, and they were paying him $600. Clara would be a "female assistant" paid only $250.

Clara was so shocked and hurt that she couldn't eat. She tried to stay on at Schoolhouse One, but only grew thinner, weaker, and more depressed, until her voice faded away. Finally, she decided that the only way to recover her health was to leave Bordentown. So in February of 1854, that is what she did.

Clara moved to Washington, DC, with her good friend Fanny Childs to make a new start. Very quickly her health and mood improved.

Through the friend of a relative, she was offered a job as a clerk at the US Patent Office. Her salary was $1,400 per year—much, much higher than her teacher's wages. In fact, she was paid as much as a man—she had insisted on it.

"My situation is delightfully pleasant," she wrote to a friend. She enjoyed copying documents at the Patent Office in her clear handwriting.

US PATENT OFFICE

THE PATENT OFFICE

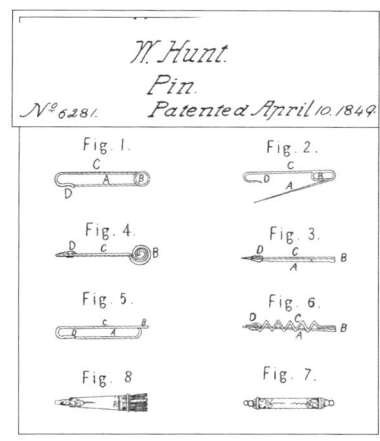

DOZENS OF THINGS WE USE EVERY DAY WERE INVENTED DURING CLARA BARTON'S LIFETIME. THEY INCLUDE THE SAFETY PIN, THE ELEVATOR, THE DISHWASHER, THE TELEPHONE, THE TYPEWRITER, THE STAPLER, DYNAMITE, TOILET PAPER, COCA-COLA, THE ROLLER COASTER, CONTACT LENSES, AND THE ZIPPER. ALL WERE AWARDED PATENTS BY THE US PATENT OFFICE, WHICH MEANT THAT ONLY THE PATENT OWNER (USUALLY THE INVENTOR) COULD MANUFACTURE AND SELL THEM. CERTAIN PROCESSES, LIKE PASTEURIZING MILK TO MAKE IT LAST LONGER, ALSO COULD BE PATENTED.

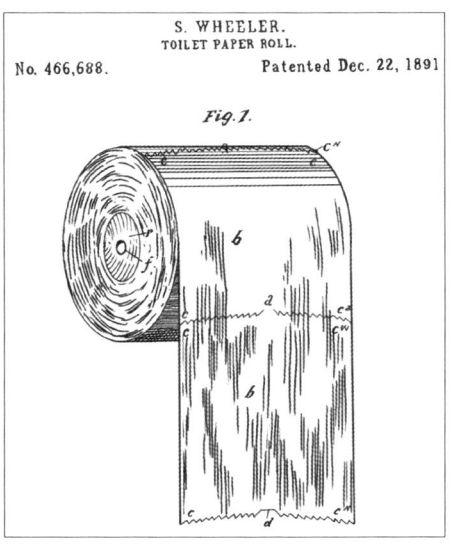

Clara loved reading in the Library of Congress. She visited the Senate, listened to debates from the gallery, and began to understand politics. And she made many new friends.

But as a New England woman and a longtime opponent of slavery, Clara was often troubled by the talk she heard in Washington. Slavery was still legal there, as it was in many Southern states.

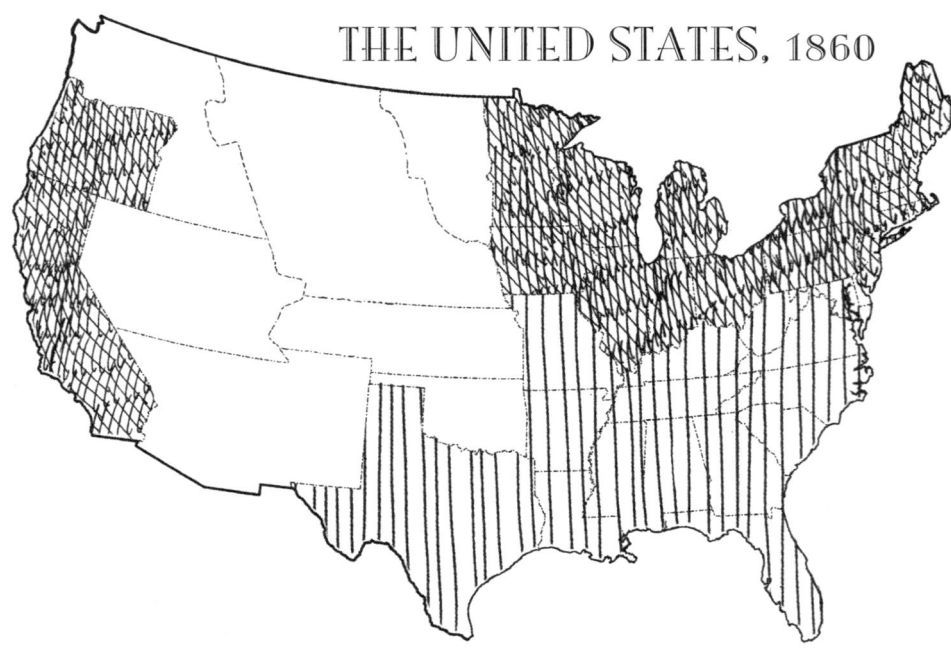

THE UNITED STATES, 1860

||||||| SLAVE STATES   FREE STATES

Southerners believed that they, not the federal government, should decide if slavery was legal or not. Opponents of slavery felt that only the Union, as the US government was called, should have the power to decide.

By 1860, the issue was tearing the country apart. Southern states were threatening to leave the Union. If they did, there would be war, and Clara dreaded it. "Men talk flippantly of dividing the Union," she wrote to her brother Stephen. "This may happen, but in my humble opinion, never until our very horses gallop in human blood."

Soon after Lincoln won the 1860 presidential election, South Carolina, Georgia, Florida, Mississippi, Alabama, Louisiana, and Texas announced that they were seceding—leaving the Union to form their own government. (Within weeks, Arkansas, North Carolina, Virginia, and Tennessee joined them.) They called their new country the Confederate States of America.

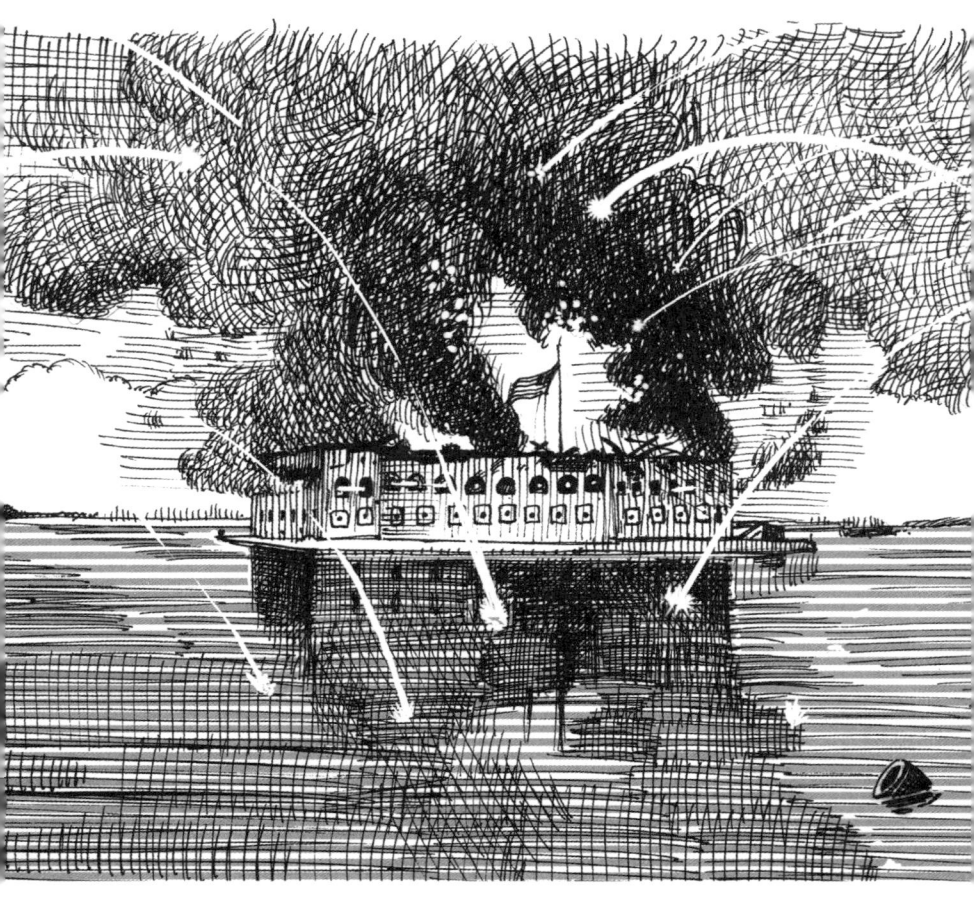

In April 1861, their men attacked Union soldiers stationed in Fort Sumter, off the South Carolina coast.

The Civil War had begun.

Chapter 4
Angel of the Battlefield

Clara's natural response to trouble always had been to pitch in and help. When war broke out, she soon found a way.

On April 19, 1861, the Sixth Massachusetts Regiment, volunteer Union troops bound for

Washington, was attacked by an angry mob in Maryland. Clara knew many of the soldiers personally from her teaching days, and hurried to their aid, bringing food and supplies she had paid for herself.

As more troops from New England gathered in and around the capital, she arranged to provide clothing, food, blankets, and other necessary items for them. A one-woman supply system, she worked tirelessly without wages. Being needed was her reward.

The taking of Fort Sumter on April 12 had

been a skirmish rather than a battle—no soldiers
were killed or even seriously hurt. However,
the first major battle of the war, at Bull Run in
Virginia, was very different. Nearly three thousand
Union soldiers were killed or wounded. Many of
them died slow, terrible deaths on the field because
there were so few doctors to treat them.

NINETEENTH-CENTURY MEDICINE

WHEN CLARA BEGAN NURSING HER BROTHER DAVID IN 1832, NOBODY KNEW THAT GERMS CAUSED INFECTION AND SPREAD DISEASE. DOCTORS DIDN'T WASH THEIR HANDS OR WEAR GLOVES WHEN THEY WORKED. THEY DIDN'T STERILIZE THEIR INSTRUMENTS. AND THEY OFTEN BLED PATIENTS WITH LEECHES, WORMS THAT FEED ON HUMAN AND ANIMAL BLOOD. LEECHING WAS SUPPOSED TO DRAW OUT THE "BAD BLOOD" THAT WAS CAUSING THE ILLNESS—THOUGH IT ALMOST NEVER DID.

MEDICINE WAS IMPROVING AT THE TIME OF THE CIVIL WAR, BUT NOT QUICKLY ENOUGH TO PREVENT MUCH TERRIBLE SUFFERING. DISEASES SUCH AS DYSENTERY, TUBERCULOSIS, SMALLPOX, AND TYPHOID FEVER SPREAD SO QUICKLY THAT MORE SOLDIERS DIED OF INFECTION AND DISEASE THAN OF ACTUAL COMBAT INJURIES.

Hearing of this, Clara wanted more than anything to nurse the wounded men herself. But that was out of the question. In those days, no respectable woman traveled alone, much less to be with groups of male soldiers.

As the war continued, the idea of traveling to the front haunted Clara. She wrote to the War Department and talked to every politician she knew. Nobody would issue her a pass—women simply did not belong on the battlefield. With so much opposition, Clara began to doubt herself. She asked her ailing father, now eighty-eight years old, what he thought.

Frail and sick as he was, Stephen Barton still could think clearly. And he had once been a soldier himself. Now he told Clara exactly what she wanted to hear: that nursing the wounded on the field would not bring her shame, but respect. It was the right thing to do.

Her father's blessing freed Clara. After his death she doubled her efforts, writing to Union generals, judges, and government officials with her request. She finally got permission in July 1862, and set up a way to transport supplies—bandages, clothing, and food—from women's groups in New Jersey and Massachusetts to Washington, DC.

A few weeks later, after the Union defeat at a battle in Cedar Mountain, Virginia, Clara made her first trip to the front. As the daughter of a soldier, she had happy memories of playing war games with her father. But the war raging around her was brutal, destructive, and all too real.

Yet Clara did her work with resolve, bringing medical supplies to field hospitals and personally caring for countless sick and wounded men. When no doctor was at hand, she used her pocket

knife to remove bullets. Ignoring cannon shells
and sniper fire, she dressed wounds, dispensed
medicine, and assisted at amputations. She closed
the eyes of the dead. She went without sleep and
gave away her food. At Antietam, one of the

bloodiest battles ever fought in the United States,
a Confederate bullet ripped through her sleeve,
killing the soldier she was tending. Seeing her
courage under fire, a Union surgeon wrote, "In
my feeble estimation, General McClellan, with all
his laurels, sinks into insignificance beside the true
heroine of the age, the angel of the battlefield."

"The whole city in gloom. No one knows what to do," Clara wrote in her diary on April 15, 1865. Just four days after the Confederacy surrendered, President Abraham Lincoln had been shot and killed. It was a tragic ending to a horrible war. As a nine-car funeral train carried Lincoln's coffin home to Illinois, Clara stayed in her apartment alone, mourning. Later, she wrote:

"From the northern ocean to the southern seas was only this.
A silence born of grief too mighty for words . . .
And thus they bore him on
And laid him in the quiet grave among his own."

Just as Stephen Barton had predicted, Clara's work at the front brought her admiration and respect. It also made her famous, and she got thousands of letters asking for her help in finding missing soldiers. With government permission, she opened an office to identify the Union soldiers who were missing or dead, and to publish their names.

MISSING SOLDIERS. OFFICE. 3RD STORY. ROOM 9. MISS. CLARA BARTON.

A former Union soldier named Dorence Atwater helped her greatly. While an inmate at the Confederacy's Andersonville prison in Georgia, Atwater had been assigned to record the names of the dead. Conditions in

DORENCE ATWATER

Andersonville were so gruesome that at least one hundred men each day died of disease, starvation, or both. Atwater feared that prison officials would not tell the truth about all the men who died there, so he kept his own secret records. He smuggled them out upon his release and got them to Clara. She helped him arrange for the list of nearly thirteen thousand names to be published, so that scores of families could finally mourn their loved ones. And when the new national cemetery in Andersonville opened on August 17, 1865, she was there to raise the flag.

Chapter 5
Speaking Out

At the end of 1865, Clara lost her job at the Patent Office. Without the job she loved, she felt lost and sad. To make things even worse, her money was running out.

Then her friend Fanny Gage came to visit. Like Clara, "Aunt Fanny," as she was called, was an outspoken, intelligent woman from New England. She had lectured widely on behalf of freed slaves. In her opinion, Clara should lecture, too.

FANNY GAGE

"Tell the world as you tell me," she urged, "the story of the battlefield—the story of soldiers' suffering."

Clara did not enjoy public speaking. Yet she turned out to be very good at it. People

throughout the Northeast and the Midwest were captivated by her clear, musical voice. Somehow it made her war stories—about wading through blood, using corn husks for bandages, and comforting the dying—even more shocking and dramatic. Union veterans, church groups, literary societies, and women's organizations flocked to hear her, and her fame grew. Hundreds of baby girls were named Clara in her honor. And in two years she earned enough money to last the rest of her life.

Clara's speaking tour also led to friendships with Elizabeth Cady Stanton and Susan B. Anthony. She agreed with them that women's suffrage—the right of women to vote—should become law. So should the right to equal pay. Memories of being denied work because she was a woman still stung Clara, and the subject became a key point in her talks. Meanwhile, Stanton and Anthony were happy to promote her lectures.

ELIZABETH CADY STANTON AND SUSAN B. ANTHONY

Clara Barton was living proof that women were every bit as courageous, intelligent, and resourceful as men.

VOTING RIGHTS FOR WOMEN

ELIZABETH CADY STANTON OF MASSACHUSETTS, MOTHER OF ELEVEN CHILDREN, WAS ONE OF THE VERY FIRST WOMEN TO SPEAK OUT ON WOMEN'S RIGHTS. IN 1848 SHE AND LUCRETIA MOTT HELPED ORGANIZE THE FIRST WOMEN'S RIGHTS CONVENTION IN SENECA FALLS, NEW YORK. EQUAL TREATMENT OF WOMEN AND MEN UNDER THE LAW,

AND VOTING RIGHTS FOR WOMEN (ALSO KNOWN AS "WOMEN'S SUFFRAGE") WERE THEIR GOALS.

THEY WENT ON TO PARTICIPATE IN THE FIRST NATIONAL WOMEN'S RIGHTS CONVENTION IN WORCESTER, MASSACHUSETTS, TWO YEARS LATER. AMONG THE THOUSAND ATTENDEES WAS SUSAN BROWNELL ANTHONY. SHE AND STANTON BECAME FRIENDS AND SOON BEGAN WORKING TOGETHER. THEY WROTE, TOURED, AND LECTURED, ATTRACTING MANY THOUSANDS OF WOMEN WHO SHARED THEIR IDEALS. THESE WOMEN BECAME KNOWN AS "FEMINISTS."

UNFORTUNATELY, EARLY FEMINISTS COULD NOT AGREE ABOUT VOTING RIGHTS. SOME THOUGHT AFRICAN AMERICAN MEN SHOULD BE GIVEN THE VOTE BEFORE WOMEN. OTHERS BELIEVED THAT WOMEN SHOULD BE FIRST. THE ISSUE DIVIDED THEM SHARPLY AND SLOWED THEIR PROGRESS.

IN 1869 ALL MEN, REGARDLESS OF RACE, WON THE RIGHT TO VOTE. AFTER MANY YEARS OF STRUGGLE, WOMEN WON IT, TOO, IN 1920.

Clara's health began to suffer during her speaking tour. She was pushing herself too hard. She kept lecturing until one spring night in 1868 when her voice suddenly gave out. Unable to speak, she was forced to cancel her engagements and go home to Massachusetts to recuperate. There the family doctor made her understand that she would not truly regain her health without

a long rest. "You can't rest in your own country. They won't let you," he said, advising her to go to Europe.

Several months later, she did.

Chapter 6
The Long Campaign

Clara had arranged to stay with family friends in Geneva, Switzerland. She hoped the clean air of the mountain city would do her good, and

it did. During her stay, a man named Louis Appia came to see her. He knew of Clara's work during the American Civil War, and told her he was a member of the newly formed International Red Cross. Clara had never heard of the group. But

LOUIS APPIA

she agreed with its goals: to help the wounded in wartime; to do so without favoring one side

over the other; and to do its
work with volunteers and
donations. The Red Cross
wanted to do what Clara had
tried to do during the Civil
War back home.

In 1864, said Appia, all the Red Cross's
member countries had signed an agreement called
the First Geneva Convention. This treaty said that
Red Cross workers were neutral (they didn't favor

one side or another during a war), and that they could help any wounded soldier without being attacked or taken prisoner. The Geneva treaty would relieve suffering and save many, many lives. The United States, however, had not signed the treaty. Why was that? he asked.

His question startled Clara. Like the snap of a hypnotist's fingers, it seemed to awaken her—and give her fresh purpose. After reading the pamphlets Appia left with her, Clara wanted very much to see the Red Cross in action.

In 1870, when the Franco-Prussian War broke out between France and Germany, Clara quickly volunteered for the Red Cross. She worked with hundreds of women in Strasbourg, France, who had been left poor and homeless by the war. Clara trained them to make and sell clothing, and before long they were supporting themselves and their families. Clara also visited Red Cross headquarters in Basel, Switzerland.

The Swiss organization ran like clockwork. Its well-stocked warehouses, and scores of trained nurses, were sharply different from her own haphazard war efforts. Clara was full of admiration for the Red Cross's "order, plenty, cleanliness, and comfort," she wrote. "As I saw all this . . . I said to myself, 'If I live to return to my country, I will try to make my people understand the Red Cross and that treaty.'"

THE GENEVA CONVENTION

IN 1859, A YOUNG SWISS MAN NAMED JEAN HENRI DUNANT PUBLISHED A BOOK CALLED *A MEMORY OF SOLFERINO*. IT DESCRIBED THE TERRIBLE SUFFERING HE HAD SEEN AFTER A HUGE BATTLE IN SOLFERINO, ITALY. DUNANT'S BOOK WAS READ ALL OVER

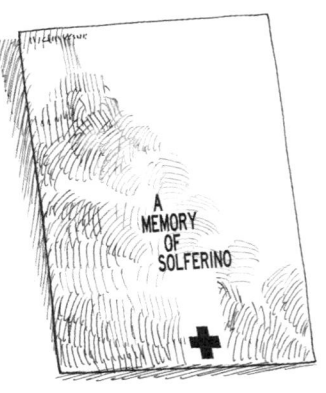

EUROPE. BY 1863 HE AND A SWISS COLLEAGUE NAMED GUSTAVE MOYNIER HAD PERSUADED MANY HEADS OF STATE TO JOIN THEIR CAUSE—A RELIEF ORGANIZATION CALLED THE INTERNATIONAL RED CROSS THAT WOULD PROVIDE HUMANE TREATMENT TO WAR VICTIMS.

ON AUGUST 22, 1864, DELEGATES FROM SIXTEEN COUNTRIES GATHERED IN GENEVA, SWITZERLAND, TO SIGN THE FIRST GENEVA CONVENTION. THE AGREEMENT, SOMETIMES CALLED THE TREATY OF GENEVA, CONSISTED OF RED CROSS GUIDELINES:

- IN WARTIME, ALL WOUNDED OR SICK SOLDIERS WOULD RECEIVE HELP.

- RED CROSS DOCTORS, NURSES, AND OTHER VOLUNTEERS, THEIR FIELD HOSPITALS AND AMBULANCES, WOULD BE NEUTRAL AND IMMUNE FROM CAPTURE.

- THE SYMBOL OF THEIR NEUTRALITY WAS A RED CROSS ON A WHITE BACKGROUND—THE REVERSE OF THE SWISS FLAG.

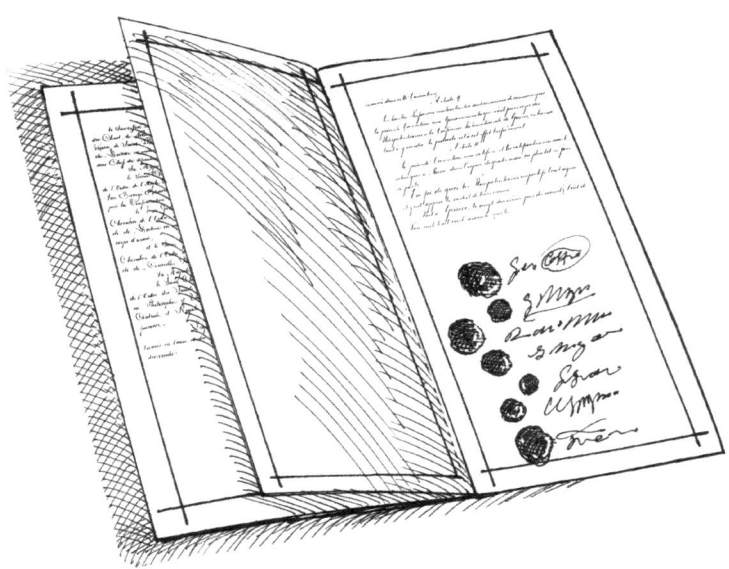

True to her word, after she returned to America, Clara began campaigning for the United States to sign the Geneva Convention. In 1878 she wrote and published a pamphlet called *The Red Cross of the Geneva Convention: What It Is.* In it, she introduced the idea of an American Red Cross that would serve victims of "national or widespread calamities, such as plagues, cholera, yellow fever, and the like, devastating fires or floods, railway disasters, mining catastrophes, etc." A group designed to help ordinary Americans during natural disasters, she argued, would do a world of good.

Clara approached old friends in Washington and even met with President Rutherford B. Hayes and his wife. The president expressed interest in the Red Cross, but passed her along

to the State Department, which ignored her.
The fact was that nearly a century after George
Washington had warned the country against
"foreign entanglements," the US government was
still unwilling to sign a treaty with European
governments. The word "International" before
"Red Cross" did not work in Clara's favor.

JAMES A. GARFIELD

Clara would not give up. She persuaded Susan B. Anthony and other feminists to support her, along with groups of Union war veterans. She made sure to win over any reporters who might help with favorable publicity. And in 1881, President-elect James A. Garfield gave her his approval.

Clara was jubilant. "After all these years of writing, hoping, and waiting," she wrote to the International Red Cross in Geneva, "I want to give you and your noble society its first word of hope." In May 1881 she began gathering together the people who would make up the first American chapter, and its members voted to make her president.

Tragically, President Garfield was shot on July 2, 1881, and died of his wounds on September 19. Clara was overwhelmed with sorrow. And though she tried, she couldn't help but fear that Chester A. Arthur, replacing Garfield as president, might oppose the Treaty of Geneva and the Red Cross.

President Arthur soon put her fears to rest. In a speech to the Senate that December, he praised

the Geneva Convention. On March 16, 1882, he signed it, making the United States the newest member of the International Red Cross. On that day, Clara won her long campaign.

Chapter 7
Fire, Famine, and Flood

The new American Red Cross (ARC) had begun quietly. No headlines announced the opening of its headquarters in Washington, DC. When the ARC sent help to Michigan, where a series of forest fires left thousands of people homeless, the press was silent. Meanwhile, local Red Cross chapters were springing up without fanfare.

The lack of attention worried Clara. She had struggled to bring the Red Cross to the United States, giving it all her energy and a great deal of her money. Now it would need even more money to keep going—much more than she had. The government refused her appeals for funding, which meant that operating expenses would have to come from private donors. For this to happen, the Red Cross needed good publicity and lots of it.

Then, in the spring of 1882, the Mississippi

River flooded—twice. The calamity destroyed homes, farms, and crops. Responding swiftly, the American Red Cross raised donations of food, clothing, blankets, and even $10,000 worth of seeds for replacement crops. Clara spent four months directing relief work. People of the region were deeply grateful and formed new Red Cross chapters in Memphis, Natchez, New Orleans, and Vicksburg.

"We are constantly gaining, both in usefulness and appreciation," Clara wrote to a friend that year.

When the Ohio River flooded in 1884 (at one point the water crested at seventy-one feet in the city of Cincinnati), the Red Cross again acted quickly. It collected donations of food, clothing,

fuel, and household items for the victims, which Clara delivered on a chartered boat. She traveled up and down the river for three months, helping many thousands of people—and attracting stellar publicity. One Chicago newspaper predicted: "The day is not far distant—if it has not already come—when the American people will recognize the Red Cross as one of the wisest and best systems of philanthropic work in modern times." Flood victims called Clara an angel and a saint. Their gratitude, and the huge donations that came in during and after the flood, made her work worthwhile.

But it did take a serious toll on her health, something Clara did not like to admit. Just as she tried to appear youthful by dyeing her graying hair and wearing makeup, she also tried to hide her frequent bouts of fatigue and depression. The Red Cross was "her child," the very center of her life. She didn't want anybody to think she was too old, or too weak, to run it. Only her very closest friends and associates knew the truth.

After the Ohio flood, Clara was too weary to run the Red Cross office in Washington, DC. She had bought a house in Dansville, New York, in 1878, and now she retreated to it, hoping for a long rest. But her time there was cut short by a request from the US Secretary of State. Would she attend the International Conference of the Geneva Convention in Switzerland on behalf of the United States? It was the first time in history that a woman had been asked to represent the United States at an international event. She just couldn't refuse.

If she was exhausted during her week in Geneva, Clara didn't show it. She attended meetings and programs, met delegates from twenty-two different countries, and spoke to the assembly about her Civil War experiences. She described the many ways the ARC had helped

out in peacetime, bringing vital aid to thousands of fire and flood victims. The Conference was so impressed with her work that it voted to follow her example. It changed the International Red Cross charter to include peacetime relief, and called it "the American Amendment" in Clara's honor.

It was a wonderful moment for Clara. During her stay in Europe she was honored many times over and came home with as many medals as a military hero.

Unfortunately, the busy trip to Switzerland took its toll, and Clara fell ill on her return to the United States. She went back to work before she was completely well, fearing that if she stayed away, the American Red Cross would fall apart. Overwork and exhaustion had often stopped her before, but she could not, or would not, find a qualified person to share her workload. In 1885, she was still the Red Cross's only full-time employee!

"Decide that I must attend to all business myself," she wrote in her diary, "and learn to do all myself."

As Clara would learn, this was not the best way to run a fast-growing national organization. But she never got around to addressing the problem. Her attempts to raise money for the Red Cross, interrupted by a string of natural disasters, kept her much too busy.

THE MOST DECORATED WOMAN OF THE AGE

EUROPEAN ROYALTY, HEADS OF STATE, VETERANS' GROUPS, PROFESSIONAL ORGANIZATIONS, AND GRATEFUL DISASTER VICTIMS HEAPED MEDALS ON CLARA. SHE WAS ALSO GIVEN DOZENS OF GEM-STUDDED BROOCHES, LOCKETS, AND PINS AS GIFTS. MANY PHOTOGRAPHS SHOW HER WEARING A LARGE AMETHYST PIN IN THE SHAPE OF A PANSY, A GIFT OF FRIENDSHIP FROM GRAND DUCHESS LOUISE OF BADEN.

CLARA NEVER WORE ALL OF HER MEDALS AND PINS TOGETHER—THERE WERE SIMPLY TOO MANY! SHE KEPT THEM IN AN OLD SATCHEL AND LIKED TO TALK ABOUT THEM WHEN ADMIRERS CAME TO VISIT HER.

SOME OF HER FAVORITES WERE:

- A DIAMOND-AND-GOLD PIN FROM THE GRAND ARMY OF THE REPUBLIC, UNION ARMY VETERANS. IT HONORED CLARA'S NURSING SERVICE DURING THE CIVIL WAR.

- THE SILVER CROSS OF IMPERIAL RUSSIA. FOR RELIEF WORK DURING THE RUSSIAN FAMINE, IT WAS PRESENTED TO CLARA PERSONALLY BY CZAR NICHOLAS II OF RUSSIA IN 1902.

- THE GENEVA MEDAL OF HONOR. THIS WAS GIVEN TO CLARA BY THE INTERNATIONAL COMMITTEE OF THE RED CROSS, AFTER THE UNITED STATES SIGNED THE GENEVA CONVENTION IN 1882.

Her longest and most difficult mission came
on May 31, 1889, with the terrible Johnstown
flood. Beginning with unusually heavy spring
rains, the flood became a full-fledged disaster

when the huge South Fork Dam in Pennsylvania
collapsed ten miles from Johnstown, releasing a
staggering twenty million tons of water. It was
one of the worst catastrophes of the century.

Whole towns were swept away, more than two thousand people were killed, and tens of thousands were left homeless.

Clara and her band of fifty volunteers set up a tent and got down to work. They called for donations, built a warehouse, and then distributed the chairs, mattresses, kitchen utensils, food, clothing, and medicine that came in from all over the country. They constructed a thirty-room "Red Cross hotel" out of lumber trucked in from the Midwest.

It was the first of many dwellings they built for the homeless. Clara even held a formal tea when the hotel opened, as if assuring people that order and comfort would soon return to their battered town.

She left after five months of grueling work, knowing that she and the Red Cross had done themselves proud.

Chapter 8
A Heart without Borders

After the Johnstown relief mission, Clara continued to run the Red Cross exactly as she liked, making most of the important decisions herself. Her stamina and determination were exceptional for someone in her seventies. Even suffering through periods of mental and physical exhaustion, she managed to do more than most people half her age. And her age was a subject she carefully avoided. It wasn't because of vanity— she had never thought herself a beauty. It was because she couldn't bear the thought that she was becoming too old to run the Red Cross.

Sadly, Clara's way of doing things had been working against her for some time. Critics resented her iron rule. They complained that she

FIRST AMERICAN RED CROSS HEADQUARTERS,
WASHINGTON, DC

never bothered to keep clear financial records.
And it was true that Clara neglected to keep
track of the money the Red Cross was spending.
Sometimes it was her own; sometimes it was from
donations. What difference did it make? The
important thing was to help.

At least that was how she felt.

In the 1890s, Clara's concern for victims of

disaster reached far beyond US borders. During the Russian famine of 1891–1892, which took hundreds of thousands of lives, she raised enough money to send shiploads of food and farming tools to Russia. She also made sure that trusted American Red Cross representatives were at the docks to unload the cargo and distribute it properly.

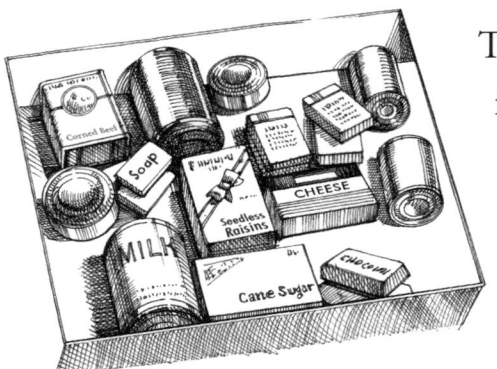

This complex, far-reaching effort saved whole villages from starvation.

At age seventy-five, Clara led a relief mission to help Armenians who were under attack in Turkey. In 1898, she and the Red Cross provided medicine, shelter, food, and clothing to thousands of Cubans when the Spanish-American War broke out. Acts like these inspired gratitude wherever Clara traveled. As she hoped, the American Red Cross was winning the respect and admiration of people all over the world.

Back at home, however, she faced all kinds of trouble. The ARC had been splitting into rival groups, with Clara's supporters on one side and her critics on the other. Her position was in jeopardy.

Then disaster struck in Texas. In September 1900, a tidal wave and flood hit Galveston, killing six thousand people in a single day and nearly destroying the town.

Clara wasted no time in organizing a relief mission. Despite how accustomed she was to catastrophe, the scene in Galveston shocked her. Hundreds of men, women, and children had been swept out to sea. Funeral pyres burned in the streets to dispose of the many dead bodies that remained.

Amid widespread despair and ruin, Clara and the Red Cross volunteers set up a workshop and storehouse in an empty building. They were soon distributing food, clothing, medicine, and household goods to the victims. The Red Cross bought over one million strawberry plants, as well as seed corn, seed potatoes, and cottonseed, for local farmers. When Clara and her volunteers left after two months, new crops were coming up, and the recovery was under way.

REPORT

OF

RED CROSS RELIEF

GALVESTON

TEXAS

Like most Americans, Clara mourned the death of President William McKinley on September 14, 1901. Of the three presidents who had been assassinated in her lifetime, he had been the kindest to her, and a solid supporter of the American Red Cross. Her health suffered when he died, and growing discord within the organization only made it worse.

Many longtime members, once loyal friends, were now openly trying to force Clara to leave. Common sense told her that she should go—she was now in her eighties, after all. But her stubborn streak, which had helped her reach so many near-impossible goals, made her hang on. She remained president of the American Red Cross until 1904.

Some ARC employees had complained to Congress about Clara, saying she had mishandled, and possibly stolen, donations of money. This personal attack was painfully humiliating. Clara had given decades of her life and much of her own money to the Red Cross. There would have been no American branch without her. Yet now the organization was doing everything it could to

cast her out. A Senate investigation found Clara innocent, but by this time she had had enough. On May 14, 1904, she resigned from the ARC and never worked for it again.

Chapter 9
Clara's Legacy

Several years before she left the Red Cross, Clara had sold her house in Dansville. In 1897 she built a home in Glen Echo, Maryland, not far from Washington, DC. It was a big, imposing place that reminded her of an ocean liner, with a wide front porch she liked to call "the main deck."

At first the house served as Red Cross headquarters and a storehouse for supplies. Then it became Clara's home when she wasn't traveling. She moved there permanently in 1904. But the move was not a retirement. At eighty-three, Clara was ready for a fresh project or two.

After many decades of nursing, she was an expert at applying first aid in an emergency. Experience had taught her that knowing the basic first-aid skills could save lives. When a colleague asked her to help set up an organization that would teach these skills to the public, Clara

was pleased to do it. The National First Aid Association was established in 1905.

Clara was appointed president of the NFAA, but she still had more time than she was used to, so she turned back to writing. Her book *The Red Cross in Peace and War* had been published in 1899 and was a hefty seven hundred pages. Now she wrote *A Story of the Red Cross: Glimpses of Field Work*, a much shorter account of her work.

Clara's last book was her most personal. In *The Story of My Childhood*, published in 1907, she describes the many good times she enjoyed on the family farm—reading poetry with her sisters, riding and shooting with her brothers, and ice skating with her young cousins. She also writes about her crippling shyness and her early fears of not fitting in.

Two days before she died, Clara dreamed she was on a Civil War battlefield, surrounded by wounded men. "I crept round once more, trying to give them at least

a drink of water to cool their parched lips," she recounted, "and I heard them . . . speak of mothers and wives and sweethearts, but never a murmur or complaint. Then I woke to hear myself groan because I have a stupid pain in my back, that's all. Here on a good bed, with every attention. I am ashamed . . ."

She died on April 12, 1912, after months of illness, with a nephew and two old friends at her side. After the funeral they traveled with her casket from Glen Echo, Maryland, to Oxford, Massachusetts, where she would be buried.

CLARA BARTON HOMESTEAD, OXFORD, MA

When their wagon driver heard he was carrying Clara's body, he dropped his reins and cried, "My God, is this the body of Clara Barton?"

Then he explained. His father, a Confederate soldier, had been shot in the neck at the Battle of Antietam. He was alone, bleeding to death. Then, said the driver, "Miss Barton found him on the battlefield and bound up his wounds in time to save his life."

Clara's journals and diaries reveal a woman who was often unhappy with herself.

Yet she kept on. She fought for equal pay for women and for women's suffrage. She made nursing a desirable profession. She worked on battlefields with the courage of a warrior. She spoke out against slavery. Her patient, single-minded efforts brought the United States into the International Red Cross. The original American Red Cross had twenty-three members; today it is part of a global network that helps close to one hundred million people every year.

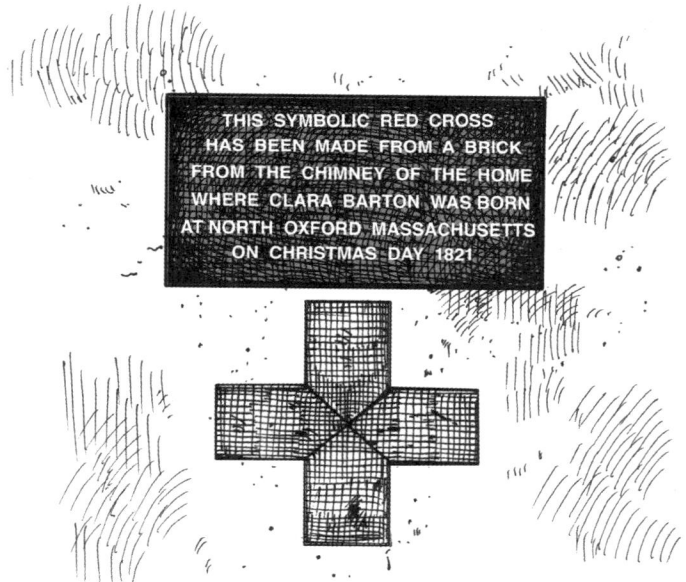

THIS SYMBOLIC RED CROSS
HAS BEEN MADE FROM A BRICK
FROM THE CHIMNEY OF THE HOME
WHERE CLARA BARTON WAS BORN
AT NORTH OXFORD MASSACHUSETTS
ON CHRISTMAS DAY 1821

Above all, she was devoted to helping people, regardless of race, religion, or nationality. Countless humanitarian groups, from Habitat for Humanity to Doctors Without Borders, exist because of Clara Barton's example. She led the way.

TIMELINE OF
CLARA BARTON'S LIFE

1821	Born December 25 in North Oxford, Massachusetts
1839	Begins teaching school in North Oxford
1845	Wins campaign to open school for children of local mill workers
1850	Attends Clinton Liberal Institute
1852	Establishes first free public school in New Jersey
1854	Moves to Washington, DC; clerks in Patent Office
1862	Nurses wounded soldiers at Second Bull Run, Fredericksburg, and Antietam
1865–1867	Helps identify more than twelve thousand missing Union soldiers
1868	Tours the northeastern United States and lectures about her war work
1870	Does relief work in France during Franco-Prussian War
1881	Founds the American Red Cross and becomes its president
1881–1900	Oversees Red Cross relief missions in Armenia, Cuba, and Russia
1902	Leads American delegation to International Red Cross conference in Russia
1904	Resigns from the Red Cross; helps form the National First Aid Association
1912	Dies April 12 in Glen Echo, Maryland

TIMELINE OF THE WORLD

Slave trade abolished in the British Empire	1833
Charles Dickens's *Oliver Twist* is published	1838
First National Women's Rights convention held in Worcester, Massachusetts	1850
Harriet Beecher Stowe's *Uncle Tom's Cabin* is published	1852
Abraham Lincoln is elected US president	1860
US Civil War begins	1861
Slavery is abolished in the United States US Civil War ends President Abraham Lincoln is assassinated	1865
Thomas Edison files the first of 1,093 successful patent applications	1868
Women in Wyoming win the right to vote	1869
Alexander Graham Bell patents the telephone	1876
President James Garfield is assassinated	1881
Statue of Liberty is dedicated in New York Harbor	1886
President William McKinley is assassinated	1901
First Russian Revolution begins	1905
The RMS *Titanic* sinks; first women's suffrage march to Albany begins in New York City	1912

BIBLIOGRAPHY

Alcott, Louisa May. **Civil War Hospital Sketches**. New York: Dover Publications, 2006.

Barton, Clara. **A Story of the Red Cross: Glimpses of Field Work**. New York: D. Appleton and Company, 1904.

Barton, Clara. **The Story of My Childhood**. New York: Arno Press, 1980.

* Dubowski, Cathy. **Clara Barton: Healing the Wounds**. Englewood Cliffs, NJ: Silver Burdett Press, 1991.

Goodwin, Doris Kearns. **Team of Rivals: The Political Genius of Abraham Lincoln**. New York: Simon & Schuster, 2005.

* Koestler-Grack, Rachel. **The Story of Clara Barton**. New York: Chelsea House, 2004.

* Krensky, Stephen. **Clara Barton: A Photographic Story of a Life**. New York: DK Publishing, 2011.

* Marko, Eve. **Clara Barton and the American Red Cross**. New York: Baronet Books, 1996.

Oates, Steven B. **A Woman of Valor: Clara Barton and the Civil War**. New York: Free Press, 1994.

Pryor, Elizabeth Brown. **Clara Barton: Professional Angel**. Philadelphia: University of Pennsylvania Press, 1997.

Pryor, Elizabeth Brown and others. **Clara Barton National Historic Site Handbook**. Washington, DC: Division of Publications, National Park Service, 1981.

Ross, Ishbel. **Angel of the Battlefield: The Life of Clara Barton**. New York: Harper & Brothers, 1956.

* Somervill, Barbara A. **Clara Barton: Founder of the American Red Cross**. Minneapolis, MN: Compass Point Books, 2007.

* Stevenson, Augusta. **Clara Barton: Founder of the American Red Cross**. New York: Aladdin Paperbacks, 1962.

* Books for young readers

* Whitelaw, Nancy. **Clara Barton: Civil War Nurse**. Springfield, NJ: Enslow Publishers, Inc., 1997

WEBSITES

"Clara Barton." National Women's Hall of Fame. www.greatwomen.org

"Clara Barton, Angel of the Battlefield," National Park Service, December 2001, www.nps.gov/clba

"Clara Barton Chronology," National Park Service, July 1998, www.nps.gov/clba

"Barton, Clara," American National Biography Online, Feb. 2000, www.anb.org

"Clara Barton." National Women's History Museum, www.nwhm.org

"Child Labor in U.S. History," Child Labor Education Project, July 2011, www.continuetolearn.uiowa.edu